BETTER LIVING
THROUGH
AIR GUITAR

BETTER LIVING THROUGH AIR GUITAR

DRAWN BY
Mr Steven Appleby

WRITTEN BY
Mr George Mole

Front Endpapers
The Dangers of Air Living
Air Guitarists fall through air windows under the
influence of imaginary Air Drugs. Do not emulate this
behaviour at home or at your place of work.

Rear Endpapers
Down to earth with a bump.

Cover Art
Our artist's rendering of legendary Finnish Air
Guitarist Teemu Pes Åpallo who claimed to have reached
nAIRvana after only 14 weeks of practice.

First published in 2005 by **Portrait**
An imprint of Piatkus Books Ltd
5 Windmill Street, London W1T 2AJ
email: info@piatkus.co.uk

Printed on paper made from timber grown in
sustainable forests according to local regulations

Set in Adobe Garamond Pro

ISBN 0 7499 5094 3

Printed and bound in Great Britain by CPI, Bath

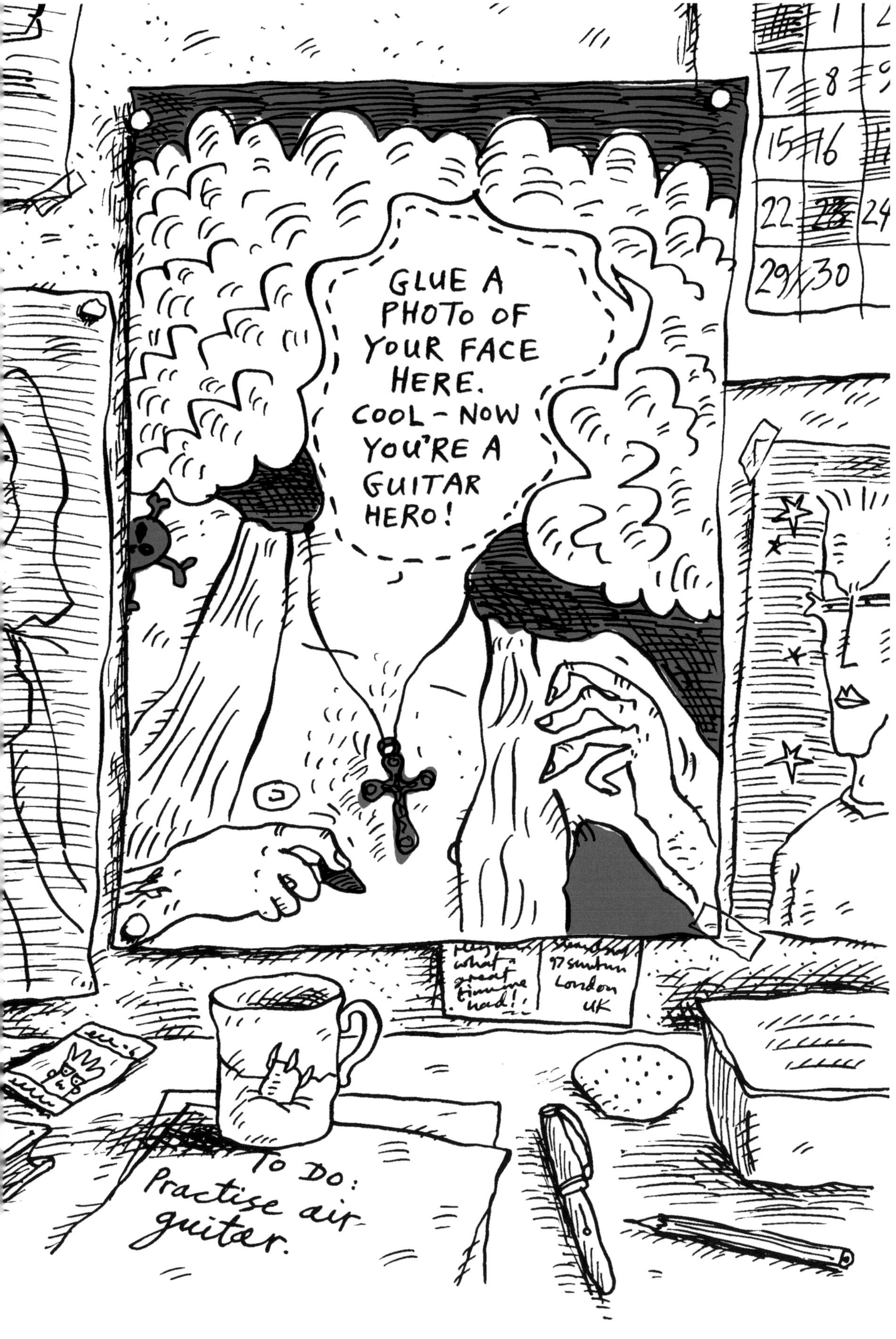
GLUE A PHOTO OF YOUR FACE HERE. COOL - NOW YOU'RE A GUITAR HERO!
London
UK
TO DO:
Practise air guitar.

Dedication...

Mr Mole intended to
dedicate this volume to his
wife, Cora, daughter, Molly,
and his Mum and Dad.
Mr Appleby, on the other
hand, had already leased the
page to his dentist, Mr Phil
Eisenberg of the
Sparklysmile Practice,
London SW22. Telephone:
0208 448 8938. Surgery open
9 am to 5.30 pm,
Monday to Friday.

After interminable negotiations
and three rounds of fisticuffs
the matter was still unsettled,
therefore this book has
NO dedication.

CONTENTS

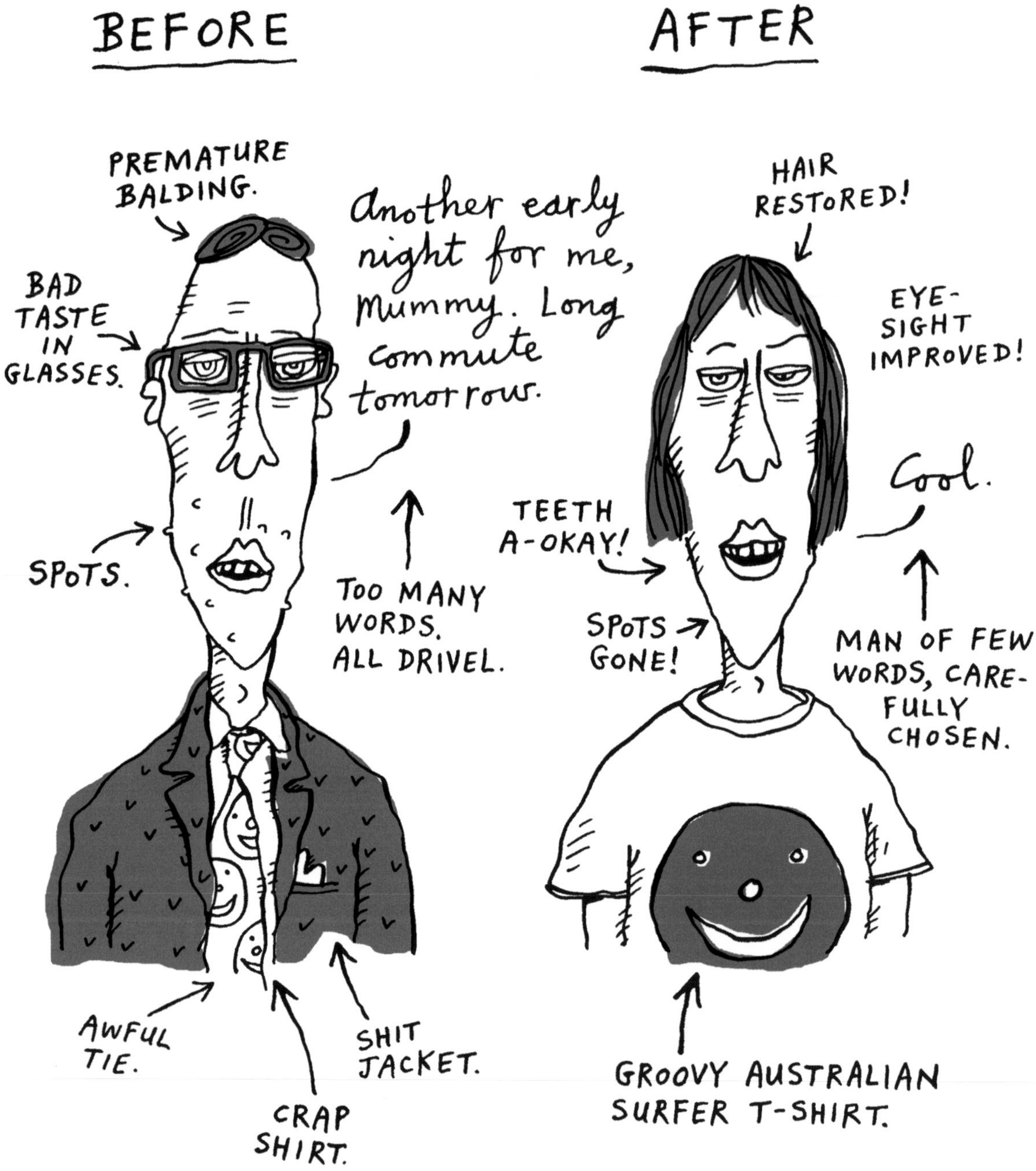
BEFORE
AFTER
PREMATURE BALDING.
Another early night for me, Mummy. Long commute tomorrow.
BAD TASTE IN GLASSES.
SPOTS.
TOO MANY WORDS. ALL DRIVEL.
AWFUL TIE.
SHIT JACKET.
CRAP SHIRT.
HAIR RESTORED!
EYE-SIGHT IMPROVED!
Cool.
TEETH A-OKAY!
SPOTS GONE!
MAN OF FEW WORDS, CAREFULLY CHOSEN.
GROOVY AUSTRALIAN SURFER T-SHIRT.

INTRODUCTION

*H*ave you been searching all your life for a hobby you can start today and be good at instantly? Well, here it is! In just a few moments you could be standing in front of your bathroom mirror playing a real Air Guitar of your very own! And it's so easy to begin! Even if you actually have some musical knowledge or skill you can still swing into action right away. And after you get going you'll want to continue for the rest of your natural life – and into the Beyond.

It's all here: the fancy moves, the cool facial expressions, the lingo, the equipment, the obscure technical details, the adulation ... It's right in front of your eyes!

But there's lots more. In this book you'll discover other kinds of Air Music and you'll learn to play all sorts of Air Instruments! Soon your health will begin to improve as unwanted weight and unsightly body hair slides off! Certain physical attributes will grow larger and any embarrassing bald spots will fill in, leaving you the body you've always wanted! Inevitably your sex life will take off as attractive people are irresistibly drawn to you and you have to satisfy them!

With all these great things happening in your life, your whole outlook will change and pretty soon you'll be feeling on top of the world!

So what are you waiting for?

Let's rock!

PART ONE

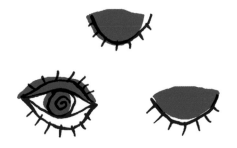

A TESTIMONIAL FROM
MR AIR GUITAR HIMSELF,
GEORGE "DWAYNE" MOLE!

Lesson One

GETTING STARTED

1 - Stand in front of a full-length mirror.

2 - Remove all tight clothing, leaving only underwear and socks.

3 - Pick up your Air Guitar. LEFT HAND holding neck (the long bit). RIGHT HAND holding body (the round bit). Unless you are Paul McCartney, in which case it's the other way round.

4 - Think of your favourite guitar solo. If you can't come up with anything try *Smoke On The Water,* which goes: duh, duh, DUH, duh, duh, DE-DUH, duh, duh, duh, DUH DUH.

5 - Now play it.

IT'S THAT EASY!

Congratulations! You're well on your way to becoming an expert.

THE ANATOMY OF AN AIR GUITARIST

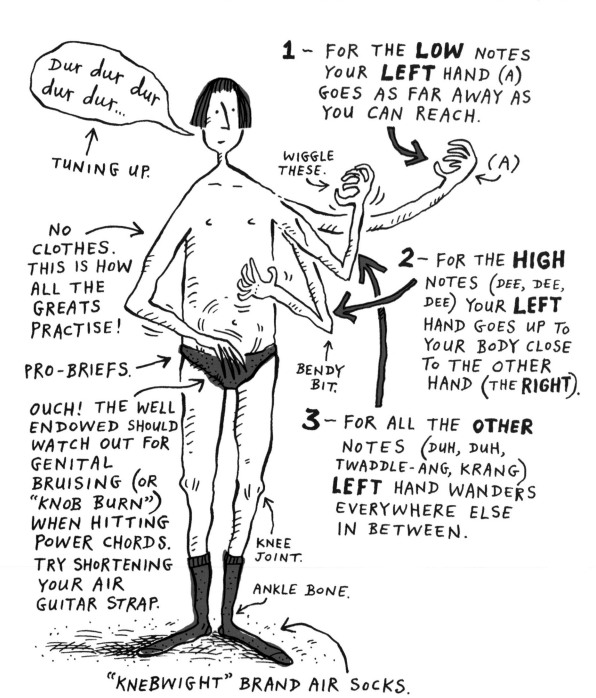

Dur dur dur dur dur...

↑
TUNING UP.

1 – FOR THE **LOW** NOTES YOUR **LEFT** HAND (A) GOES AS FAR AWAY AS YOU CAN REACH.

WIGGLE THESE. →

(A)

NO CLOTHES. THIS IS HOW ALL THE GREATS PRACTISE!

2 – FOR THE **HIGH** NOTES (DEE, DEE, DEE) YOUR **LEFT** HAND GOES UP TO YOUR BODY CLOSE TO THE OTHER HAND (THE **RIGHT**).

PRO-BRIEFS. →

BENDY BIT.

OUCH! THE WELL ENDOWED SHOULD WATCH OUT FOR GENITAL BRUISING (OR "KNOB BURN") WHEN HITTING POWER CHORDS. TRY SHORTENING YOUR AIR GUITAR STRAP.

3 – FOR ALL THE **OTHER** NOTES (DUH, DUH, TWADDLE-ANG, KRANG) **LEFT** HAND WANDERS EVERYWHERE ELSE IN BETWEEN.

KNEE JOINT.

ANKLE BONE.

"KNEBWIGHT" BRAND AIR SOCKS.

THE MUSIC

*I*t's whatever you're listening to! Whatever is digitized, whatever is in the vinyl, whatever rocks your world! Clapton, Hendrix, Richards, Zabalza! Let the music flow through you like water. Channel the music. You are the conduit, the muddy river, the rocky stream bed, the toxic flow. Let the music express you! Take what the originators gave you and release it! Break those vinyl bonds, open that electronic prison, crank it up* and LET THE MUSIC OUT!

Just make sure you credit the original artists whenever possible.

---

*Be careful when using headphones or amplification equipment in an enclosed space such as a bedroom, small car, bathroom or wardrobe.

TELLING IT LIKE IT IS

*O*f course, you can listen to your favourite solo on the electronic medium of your choice. That is cool. You know what you like ... BUT try this: make your own guitar sounds! It's true! You can replicate the exact tone of the guitar solo lodged deep in your unconscious! This means you can play Air Guitar anywhere, anytime, any way you like it! Imagine the freedom! You are UNPLUGGED! This is the true essence of Air Guitar! The ultimate! You are the master or mistress of your musical destiny!

Searching for the right sound is the Holy Grail of Air Guitar. You can spend a lifetime perfecting your sound but here are a few tried and true suggestions:

 Da, da, da – Simple but effective. Works anywhere, anytime.

 Doh, doh, doh – Good for deeper notes. Still simple, still effective.

 Duh, duh, duh – Still simple but a little funkier, too. A little more rock 'n' roll. Time to get down and dirty!

 ***Dvv, Dvv, Dvv*** – Try this through clenched teeth. Oh yeah ... Super funky (see *Facial Expressions* on page 21). Works great with hunched shoulders.

Bow, bow, bow – Not like a dog! Try it with a little nasal twang. Mmm ... This is the sound of Country Rock Air Guitar. You're channeling Fanny Smith's classic screech of pain *No Man Gonna Spread My Jam!* Uncanny.

 ***Bew, bew, bew*** – Has an exotic sound but can be real easy rockin', too.

 ***KRANG*** – Reserve this for a huge arm-swingin' chord. Also try: ***KRRRSSSS ...*** – The static-like late-night crackle of white noise on blank TV screens. Watch out – you're dribbling.

 ***Weeoo, weeoo, weeoo*** (also ***wah-oo, wah-oo, wah-oo, wicker wicker wicker*** and ***wahwahwahwah***) – Obviously this is great for echo sounds and wahwah pedal but try it with other effects, too. Maybe fuzz box or flanger. Even fatface. Waa hoo! We're rockin' now!

 Twaddleangrang, dang, dang, dang, dang, dang, dang! – Oh yeah, you've guessed it! Dueling banjoes! You are good.

 ***Nananananananana*** – Can't forget that great punk sound. This is best shouted at the highest decibel level your lungs can manage. DON'T try this with DOOFUS or EASY! But DO try it with ORGASM, VOMIT, CONSTIPATION (careful, please) and FINGER-IN-THE-MOUSETRAP (see *Facial Expressions* again).

BASS SOUNDS:

 ***Bluh bluh bluh*** – Slap those lips together, baby! You can also try this on your Classical Axe for Air Flamenco – pass the sangria, amigo ¡Que bueno!

Budda, budda, budda – The classic! Start and finish right here, you do not need to pass go.

CHOOSING YOUR INSTRUMENT

*T*he impetuous novice Air Guitarist may well be tempted to jump up and start thrashing away oblivious to the condescending smile on the face of the expert looking on. What the expert knows is that it's well worth doing some proper research before starting to flail away at any old thing. You want your Air Guitar to give years of reliable and solid service. Almost everyone aspires to owning one of the classic Air Guitars shown below. See if you can match the partial titles to the correct image!

A – The Air Strato ...   B – The Air Les P ...   C – The Air Fl ... g-V

D – The Air Twin ... 12-str ... & 6-str ...

But why not break the mould? Go on, live it up and splash out on a genuine Appleby & Mole instrument, hand-crafted by disadvantaged youth in one of our many international workshops. (Previously owned instruments are often available – log onto airyfairygodmother.com for details.)

a: The Basic – formerly sold under the title "The Willing Student." A great starter instrument at an affordable price.

b: The Manzanilla – take your flamenco to a new level ¡Si, Senor!

b.

c: The **48-string Strumathon Magma** – for when you need that industrial folk sound.

c.

d: The Cosmic Starship – cruise the universe on this stellar smoothy. This is living!

d.

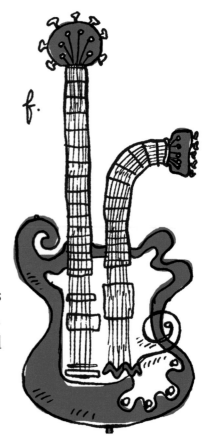

f.

f: The Flying Jumbo – formerly sold as "The Bad Boy". No fatter sound on the market!

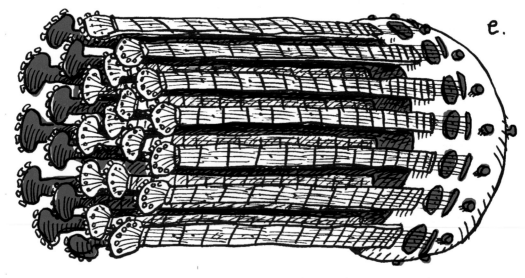

e.

Also available: the twenty-six-neck **Octoleviathon (e)** – this interesting air curio from bygone times has a great sitar sound. Add some extra air arms and fingers with our cosmetic air surgery – non-reversible, please choose responsibly. Only available to those 17 years old and under.

PICK 'N' MIX

*A*lternatively, why let yourself be restricted? There's no limit to the imagination. You can pick whatever look and attributes suit you best. We call this **Frankenstylin'** – a tried and true technique that has been used in therapy for many decades now. Developed in the 1960's to redesign parents and authority figures, it can really help you zero in on your core personality and self-manifestation by crystallizing your Air Persona.

Construct your dream instrument right here by making your very own "flip-book".

Simply cut the following 6 pages along the dotted lines, then mix up the different bits and bobs from each guitar drawing (fret board/end bit/fat bit, etc.) until you have exactly the Air Guitar that cries out to the guitar hero or heroine in you!

Now, VISUALISE … That's good. You are implanting your ideal instrument deep into your psyche. Close your eyes and – voila! There she is. Or he, in the event that you mixed the Onslaughter Sunburst V with the Godbolter "Phasmo" Barbarian.

Your choice of guitar is an excellent indicator of your character; in fact, about 17% more accurate than your horoscope. **Frankenstylin'** is also a great way to reveal the character of your potential mate. Who can resist creating their very own made-to-measure instrument? Leave the book open at these pages and see what type of guitar your mate chooses to construct. To help you, we've labeled each guitar section with its *human character insight*. You'll soon know what kind of person is sharing your toothpaste.

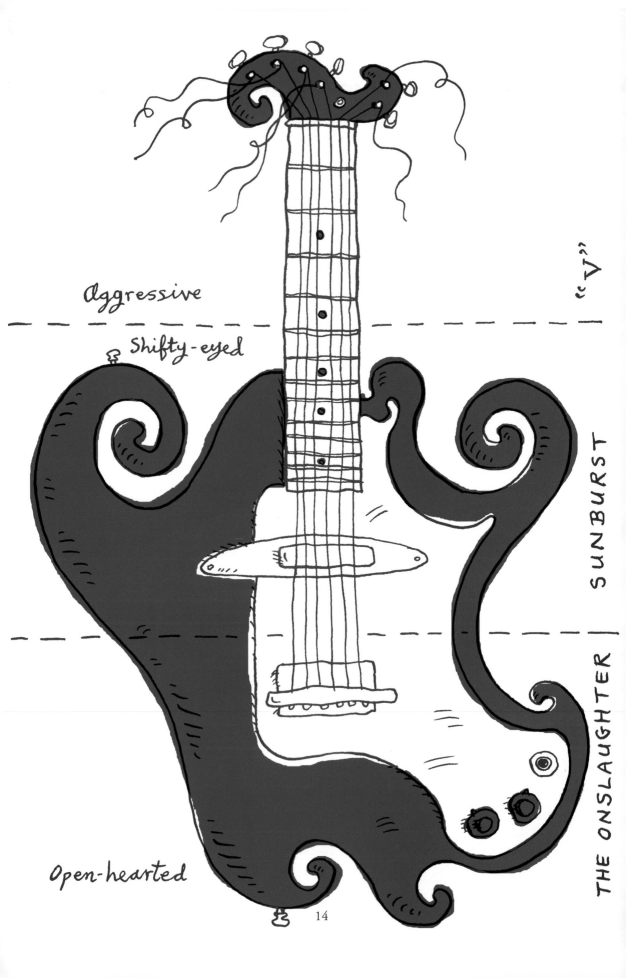

Aggressive

Shifty-eyed

Open-hearted

"V"

SUNBURST

THE ONSLAUGHTER

14

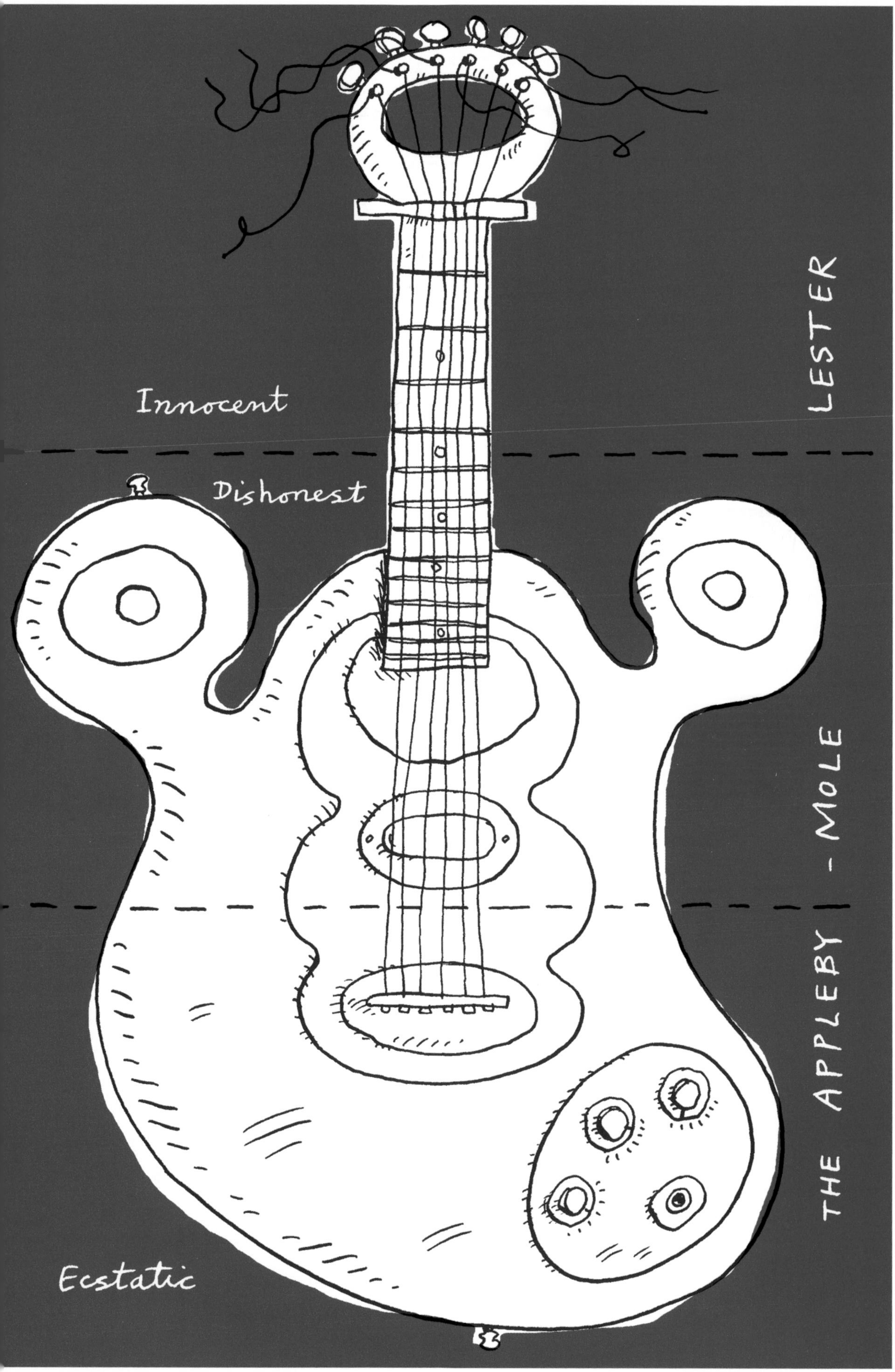
Innocent
Dishonest
Ecstatic
THE APPLEBY - MOLE LESTER

Passive

Tormented

Impulsive

BARBARIAN

"PHASMO"

THE GODBOLTER

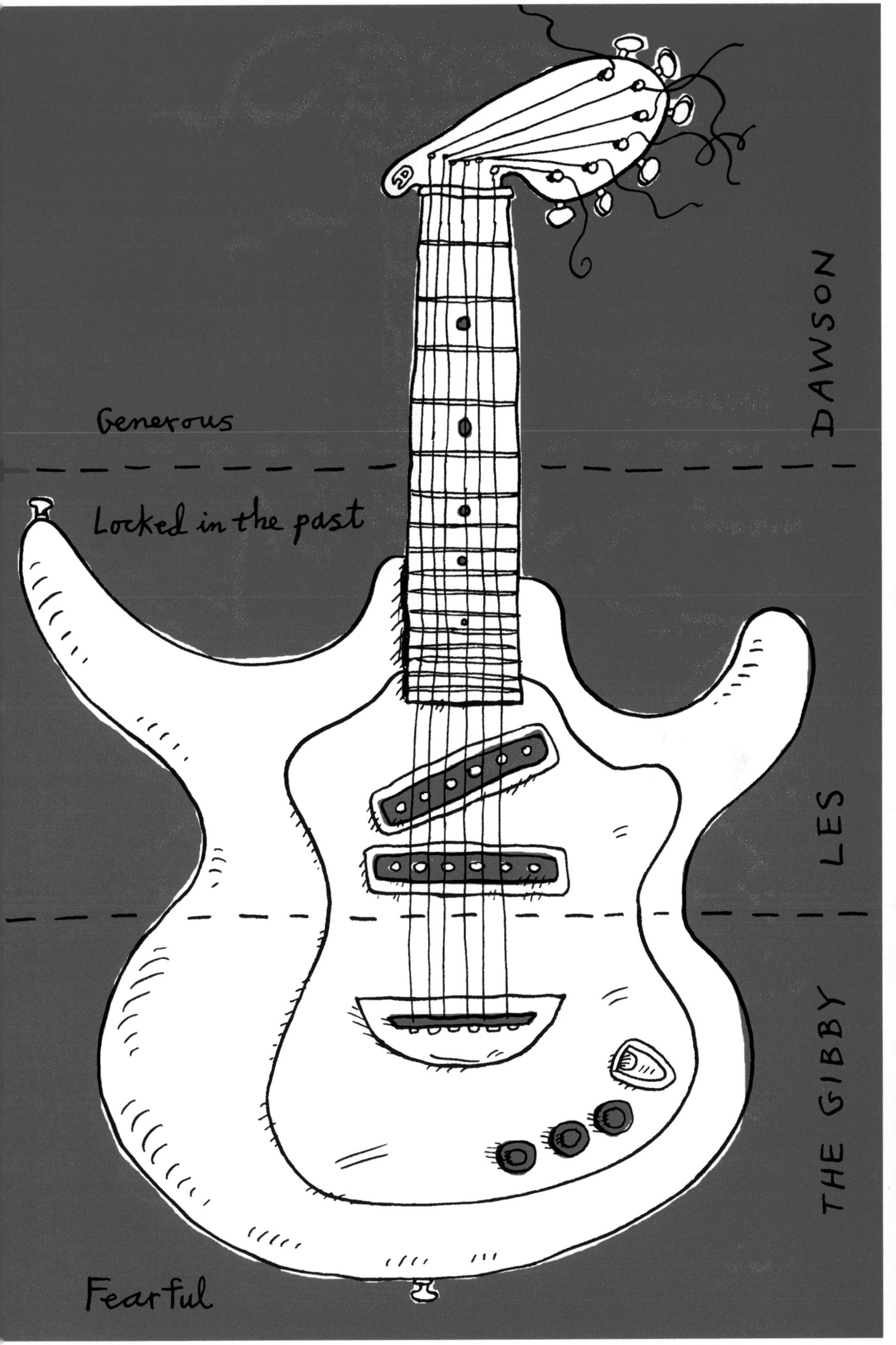
THE GIBBY LES DAWSON
Generous
Locked in the past
Fearful

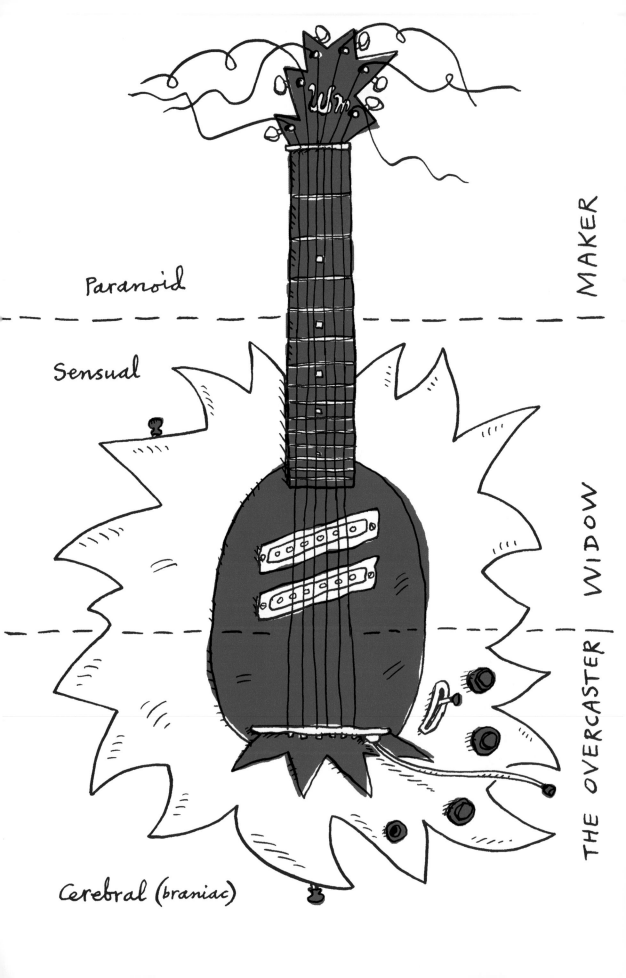

Paranoid

Sensual

MAKER

WIDOW

THE OVERCASTER

Cerebral (braniac)

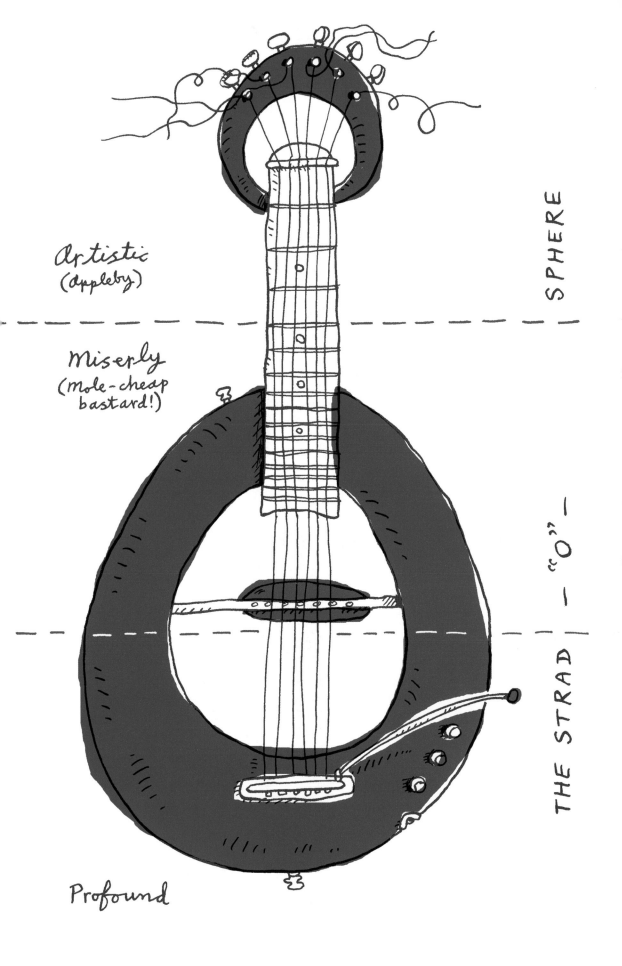

Artistic
(appleby)

Miserly
(mole-cheap
bastard!)

Profound

SPHERE

— "O" —

THE STRAD

LOOKING AFTER YOUR INSTRUMENT

*Y*our Air Guitar is a precision-engineered piece of equipment and will last you a lifetime if treated with care. Don't just sling it under the bed and **never** lean it against a radiator: the Air Glue could melt. We suggest buying a strong protective case, such as one of the ones shown below, because your Air Guitar is valuable! A 1939 Maudlin Meanderer semi-acoustic recently fetched over £12,000 on eBay. Of course, Maudlin only made a very few instruments before alcoholic dementia and advanced syphilis inspired him to become an architect.

CARBON FIBRE **STRUMATHON MAGMA** CASE. COMBINES STRENGTH, LIGHTNESS AND BEAUTY.

THE POCKET GIANT ™ CASE FOR FOLDING AIR GUITARS, SUCH AS THE MOLE & APPLEBY **FOOT LOOSE** BATTERY-POWERED ACOUSTIC.

SOLID STEEL CASE FOR STRENGTH AND HEAVINESS.

Lesson 3

FACIAL EXPRESSIONS

*T*o play great Air Guitar, or any other instrument, you have to have the right facial expression. How are people going to know if you're playing a really hard bit if you don't show it? How are they going to know it's really beautiful if you don't "telegraph" it? The audience has absolutely no idea, so it's all up to you. Here's how to do it:

THE SMUG – try thinking of something no one else knows about. Something that will make an ex-lover, authority figure, member of the Cabinet look really stupid if anyone ever finds out.
DIRE STRAITS, Sultans Of Swing.

THE CONSTIPATION – lift upper lip to expose teeth. Bear down as if eliminating solid waste. Be careful.
May we suggest BON JOVI's Livin' On A Prayer.

THE KNOWING SMILE – same thing, now close your eyes and smile. Really smile!
Pick out something by COLDPLAY.

THE HAIRBALL – lean head forward, open mouth wide and imagine silently coughing.
A great companion for LED ZEPPELIN's Black Dog.

21

THE VOMIT – as above, but close eyes and imagine serious abdominal pain. *We'd have to go with DEEP PURPLE's Smoke On The Water.*

THE ORGASM – open eyes and mouth super wide. Simulate the moment of ecstasy. Use liberally during solos. Make it your own! *Works with any mirror: GUNS N' ROSES' Sweet Child O Mine.*

THE SEX GOD – as above, but close eyes and imagine serious pelvic disturbance (see VOMIT). *ERIC CLAPTON, Layla.*

THE FUNKY – press bottom lip against upper teeth, as if about to utter an expletive.

GEORGE CLINTON, EARTH, WIND & FIRE, JAMES BROWN... Basically, go through the vinyl your uncle has been storing in the garage ever since the divorce in '82.

THE SUPER-FUNKY – as above, but close eyes, hunch shoulders and raise upper lip, as if about to utter an expletive during a nightmare.

An obvious choice: RICK JAMES' Super Freak.

THE BERG – raise both eyebrows. Twice as cool! Try closing both eyes too! Ultra cool! *Anything by KING CRIMSON.*

THE COOL – raise one eyebrow, while projecting a confident, even cocky attitude. Great for Jazz Air Guitar! *STEELY DAN's Kid Charlemagne.*

THE WATERMELON – a deceptive look. Mouth the words as if singing along. Mostly used for easy listening rock 'n' roll, but can be adapted for any style and looks great with a foreign language. And if you don't know, or can't understand the words, just keep repeating "Watermelon, watermelon, watermelon," in time to the music. Go on, try it in front of your mirror! Looks pretty convincing, eh?

Try it out on THE FACES' Maggie Mae. A great start for this versatile expression.

THE BLAND – a great look for a hardened pro! Been there, played that. Super look for the older country session guy. Goes great with a grey ponytail or a D.A. haircut. *THE EAGLES' Hotel California.*

THE STINSON – this says "It's difficult, it's serious and I'm bringing it on to you." Very good for hard drivin' rock 'n' roll and especially for Classical Air Guitar. Don't worry we'll discuss classical music later on!

THIN LIZZY's Whisky In The Jar.

THE EGGS OVER EASY – "We're havin' a good time here. We're rockin' but it's fun!" Women dig it. Make no mistake, you'll be flypaper for the chicks.

Z Z TOP's Sharp Dressed Man.

THE DOOFUS – also known as **THE FOLKIE** or **THE GORMLESS**. Try looking happy for no reason. The perfect look with baggy clothes and an unfashionable haircut. Very political.

THE GRATEFUL DEAD's Box Of Rain.

THE FLOW – just let it be. Almost any emotion can be used: anger, sadness, lust, despair, furtive desire, panic, even boredom – although boredom overlaps with bland, try to keep your looks clean – just let that powerful emotion REGISTER on your face as you play. *Emulate the late, great Stevie Ray Vaughan molesting some innocent instrument.*

24

BASS FACE

We haven't mentioned Air Bass players, yet. This is a fascinating sub-culture. Actually, many Air Guitarists consider Air Bassists subhuman and beneath contempt. Such prejudice has no place in this book, even if bass players are often intellectually challenged. Most of them don't realise they only have four strings.

THUMBIN' ON EMPTY – a vacuous smile, head bobbing in time to the beat, or even slightly behind the beat. Try to erase all thought from your brain. For most bass players this is easy.

NIRVANA's Lithium (This suggestion does not constitute a prescription or diagnosis).

FUNKAY MONKAY – purse your lips and lay down a funky back beat.

Try WAR's Low Rider. Ask your uncle again.

SOME USEFUL EXERCISES:

HOLD EACH ONE FOR 30 SECONDS.

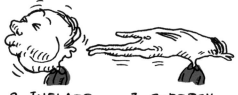

1 - INHALE. 2 - INFLATE. 3 - STRETCH. 4 - RELAX...

Try out these faces in front of your mirror after a bath or shower. Your facial muscles need to be supple and warm before you attempt some of the more challenging expressions. At last year's Air Guitar Championship, Irgun Rockwell pulled a cheek muscle and had to drop out early.

When you think you've mastered the individual expressions, try fitting a few together:

Smug-constipation-hairball – Granite-hard rock 'n' roll!

Funky-super funky-orgasm-sex god-vomit – Imagine a close-up in the video!

Bland-cool-easy-stinson-berg – Very jazz!

Bland-knowing smile-smug-doofus-watermelon – Heartwarming, sincere guy who's going to get laid tonight!

Then go with the *FLOW* with *anger-love-lust-panic!*
How about *happy-sleepy-pain-relief!*
Or try *paranoia-confidence-triumph-humility!*

Oops...

POING!

OH DEAR. A BROKEN AIR GUITAR STRING. BUT DON'T WORRY. YOUR IMAGINARY ROADIE* WILL RUSH OUT AND HAND YOU YOUR SPARE AIR GUITAR.

*See GROUPIES AND ROADIES, pages 74 & 75

Lesson 4

THE MOVES

*I*t's time to move around! You've got your game face and you've got your sounds, now try these shapes and moves. Let the picture tell your body where you want to go, because as the Man once said, "A picture is worth a thousand words." (Or in Mr Appleby's case, probably about eleven.)

THE STAGGER

THE STROLL   THE STRUT

THE STORK (not to be confused with THE STALK. To help with your balance, pick a spot about five feet in front of you and focus on it.)

THE STALK

THE STADIUM WALKABOUT (great for your girlfriend's living room, but don't get caught!)

THE EASY ACOUSTIC (long hair and beard, guitar held low)

THE ACOUSTIC (short hair, standing still, guitar held high)

THE WINDMILL (great for a really good KRANG!)

THE DUCK WALK (Chuck Berry has patented this move and all applications for its performance should be referred to his legal representatives)

ADVANCED MOVES

WARNING – do not try these at home without a qualified friend!

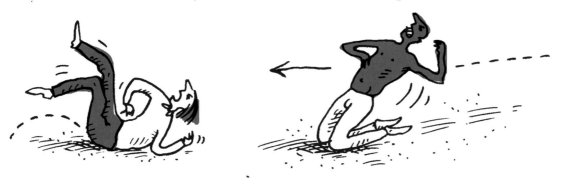

THE BIZZIE BEE

THE MUDSLIDE SLIM

fig 2 —

THE DORTMUND, or HAPPY LANDING

fig b —

Damn! Air audience
stepped out of
the way.

oof!

SMACK!

HAND JIVIN'

Try a few of these authentic hand moves:

WRISTY – show them that chord is really hard.

ONE FINGER – hold that note! Shake your head from side to side!

VIBRO – make that string whine!

SPEEDY SPIDER – how can he play that fast?

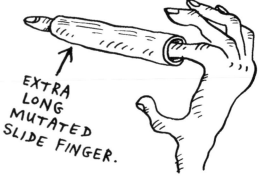

EXTRA LONG MUTATED SLIDE FINGER.

PICK IT – use your air pick like you mean it!

THE SLIDE – that slide guitar sound is great for when you feel the blues.

PART TWO

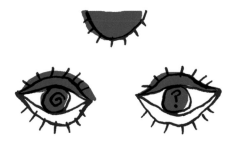

AIR GUITAR - THE FLOW CHART

You've completed the lessons, now it's time to plan an evening of Air Entertainment!

Set date and time

Disconnect phone and email

Seal letterbox

Draw curtains

Let cat out

Lock dog in bedroom with a supply of treats

Lock front door

Turn up the heat

Uncork a nice vintage

Unscrew cheap alcohol

Make a pot of tea

TAKE OFF ALL CLOTHES

Put cat out again

CHOOSE MUSIC

Dress in evening wear

Put on air underwear

Find wig. Squeeze into leather

Put cat out yet again

ROCK OUT!

WIG

VINYL TROUSERS

Acknowledge applause

Get dressed

Change into pajamas

Remove wig. Repair damage

TURN ON TV or Radio 3

Go to bed with a mug of hot chocolate

Prepare response to question: *"What did you do tonight?"*

To flatmate: (nonchalantly) *"Oh, nothing much."*

To parents: (sullen indifference at their existence) *"Nothing."*

To Loved One: (gazing into their eyes) *"Nothing of any value. But now that you're back my life can resume again."*

Welcome home, dear.

what did you do tonight?

(Feel guilty, slightly soiled – yet fulfilled)

REAL LIFE AIR GUITAR

*D*on't think for one minute that Air Guitar is just a man's game. Oh, no. These rare photographs of air country singer Fanny Smith prove otherwise. Or they would if Fanny had agreed to appear in this book, which she didn't. The uncanny lookalike on these pages is Mr Appleby, who was bullied into impersonating Ms Smith by Mr Mole, who also took the pictures. Anyway, the point is that Air Guitar isn't macho! It appeals to man, boy, male, female, and man-in-frock alike! Of course, Mr Appleby has no idea these pictures have been sneaked into the book. Mr Mole assured him they would be destroyed.

Fig a: Here's Mr A – I mean Fanny – playing Air Fiddle. Just look at those fingers fly!

Fig b: Now she's strumming the opening bars of her 1979 classic *More Of A Man Than My Man.*

Fig c: Don't forget a polite air bow – or curtsy – at the end of your set. Always treat your imaginary audience with the respect they deserve.

Fig d: Oops. Careful with your instrument, Mr A.

Fig e: Ha ha ha. Oh dear, he's looking a bit annoyed ...

Fig f: Keep back! It's just a bit of fun ... Help! No! Ow! Ouch ...

THEY ALSO SERVE WHO MERELY STAND AND STRUM

*T*he vast majority of Air Guitar players play lead. This is just a fact of life. We've all heard the phrase: "Too many chiefs and not enough Indians." Well, there are very few Native Americans playing Air Guitar and that needs to change. In the rock concert of the mind we can all play lead, but once in a while we should take off the feathered headdress, pick up the rhythm guitar and rock out. It's a good idea to be a team player, especially if that team player is providing the hard driving riffs so the lead can soar.

Take a back seat. Stand at the back of the stage. Be that other guy, with the name no one can remember. The truth is that the rhythm guitarist gets the same number of groupies. In fact, generally more. In a recent survey of top rock bands it was discovered that rhythm guitarists entertained an average of 3.4 groupies per concert whereas the lead guitarist received a meagre ration of 2.1.

TWANG-A-LANG-A-LANG...

DULL BUT DEPENDABLE.

RHYTHM GUITARIST IS THE PERFECT BAND ROLE FOR YOUR YOUNGER BROTHER.

So tonight why not try playing rhythm on a few tracks? It's relaxing: you don't have to kill yourself with all those solos. It's better for your health: the spotlights are not so blinding at the back of the stage and the stacks are further away. It's a lot more social: you can talk to the drummer and the sexy backing singers between numbers. And it's better for your sex drive (see above). Give your ego a break and let someone else wear the feathers for a change. You'll thank yourself.

AN AIR BAND JAMMING IN BEZ's DAD's GARAGE.

AIR QUIZ

1 - Which one is the rhythm guitarist?

2 - Who is out of time?

3 - Which Air Musician would rather be playing Air Jazz than Air Heavy Rock?

4 - How many Air Microphones can you count?

5 - Is the keyboard player using a Hammond organ or synthesiser?

6 - Which one is Bez?   (Answers on page 88)

THE HISTORY OF AIR MUSIC

Blind Lemon Pledge (bluesman)

"We wuh so po', I couldn' affor' no instrumen'. So I done invented de Air Guitar. Dat was my ideah. And now de done stole my ideah. Now I ain't even got my own Air Guitar."

Blind Lemon Pledge may claim to have invented Air Guitar, but Air Music has been with us since before the Dawn of Time.

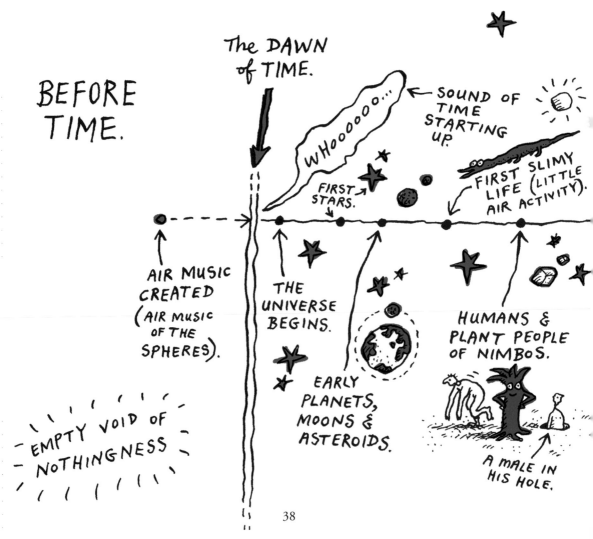

Air Guitar is merely the latest in a tradition stretching back through Air Ukelele, Air Sousapohone, Air Bagpipes, to Air Lute and Air Crumhorn. In the Victorian Alpert Museum there is a tapestry showing musicians playing Viol-Airs. In Africa skeletons of our apelike ancestors have been found still grasping their Air Banging Bones. A cave painting in Provence shows early man playing Air Rock. In Finland the fully preserved corpse of an Air Harp player was found in a peat bog crushed by a white mammoth, while in Ancient Egypt Pharaohs were buried with Air Lyres.

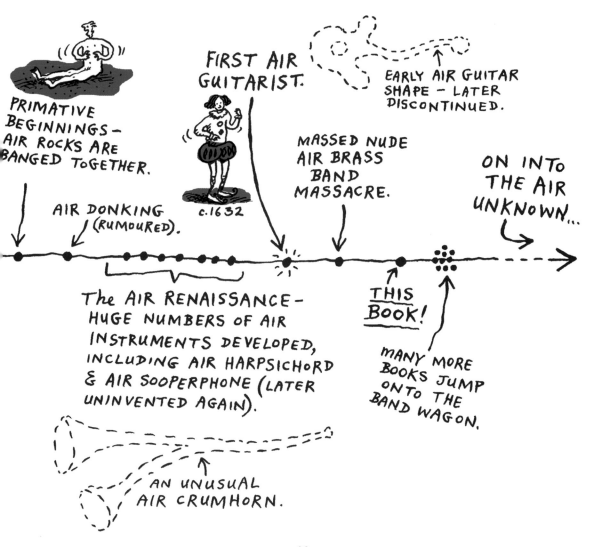

The AIR TIMELINE:

PRIMATIVE BEGINNINGS – AIR ROCKS ARE BANGED TOGETHER.

FIRST AIR GUITARIST.

c.1632

EARLY AIR GUITAR SHAPE – LATER DISCONTINUED.

MASSED NUDE AIR BRASS BAND MASSACRE.

ON INTO THE AIR UNKNOWN...

AIR DONKING (RUMOURED).

The AIR RENAISSANCE – HUGE NUMBERS OF AIR INSTRUMENTS DEVELOPED, INCLUDING AIR HARPSICHORD & AIR SOOPERPHONE (LATER UNINVENTED AGAIN).

THIS BOOK!

MANY MORE BOOKS JUMP ONTO THE BAND WAGON.

AN UNUSUAL AIR CRUMHORN.

39

By the eighteenth century Air Academies trained players in all the Air Instruments of the day. Here we see an Air Chamber Orchestra playing a Strauss waltz at the Air Symposium Musicarum held at the Great Exhibition of 1889.

But it was the twentieth century that saw Air Music really come into its own with Air Jazz, Air Swing, Air Boogey, Air Woogey and Air Bop. Throughout the 1930's musicians like Blind Lemon Pledge and Sonny Dey kept alive the flame of Air Guitar in the Deep South. Then early one morning Air Blues and Air Country fused in the primusical ooze and early Air Rock 'n' Roll crawled out of the Delta onto dry land.

Those early Air Rockers seem so staid and stiff compared to today's leading exponents of the genre, the Air Death Metal Guitarists, Air Thrash, and Air DJs with their air decks. But we digress.
As the craze jumped the Atlantic and took hold in Europe, regional differences began to appear. In France, Air Saxophone players stick one thumb in their mouth instead of simply holding the instrument. In Germany, Air Guitarists tend to

A SWINGING 60's CHICK DOES THE TWIST IN AN AIR MINI SKIRT.

play a far smaller version. But it was from the clubs of Liverpool that the British Air Invasion was launched. It started with skiffle then came Merseybeat which merged with the psychedelic sound of Carnaby Street. The Union Jack dominated the Air Music of the 60's and 70's. Every Rock God played tribute to Empire where the Music never set. Even the Americans were forced to bow down in homage. And it is from that time that the style of Air Guitar as we know it today began to crystallize: the roar of the crowd, the interminable solos, the huge hair, the bulging spandex, the willing groupies, the faithful roadies, this is where it all started. Even the holy icons of Air Guitar date from that time: the Stratocaster, the Jack Daniels, the bandana, the rolling papers ... who doesn't still cherish those

AN AIR SOUSOPHONIST COLLAPSES FROM OXYGEN STARVATION.

essential Rock-cessories? And then, Air Punk shattered the bloated domination of the Supergroups. And so, Air Guitar moved on to the next chapter ...

And what about the rest of this fair globe? Throughout the pantheon of World Music Air Instruments have been revered. The Air Sitar Players of India are often memorialized in Mughal paintings. During the Ottoman Empire Air Oud players became more important than the musicians actually playing the Oud. An Oud player was hidden behind a screen while a gorgeously attired Air Oud performer delighted the Sultan and his harem. Yusuf Ibn Ayub himself said, "We love to see the howling jackal and the niddering sand rat but an Oud is best left to the imagination." In Japan there are woodblock prints of Air Shamisen players and the geishas who served them. In 1679 real musicians rose up and massacred the Air Shamisen and Air Koto performers, sliced up

AIR OUD PLAYERS ARE
PUT TO DEATH WITH
AIR SCIMITARS.

their remains and fed them to the carp that swam in the water beneath the Floating World.

AN AIR DIDGERIDOO. NOTICE THE EXTENSIVE AND INTRICATE PATTERNING ON THE STEM.

And in primitive cultures Air Music has long been an essential part of ritual healing and magic – see *HEALTH BENEFITS*. During early Western contact with Australasian natives explorers were bemused by the extensive use of Air Digeridoo.

The history of Air Instruments is long and fascinating. Dr Julian Fantone Phd sums up the importance of the genre:

"As an evocation of apocryphal simulacra, the Air Guitar functions as a form of almost infinite fiduciary retribution. Retrograde and yet at the same time revolutionary, even rebellious in its adoption by both the cognoscenti and hoi polloi, any attempt to quantify or catalogue its true meaning is rendered interstitially redundant. Bridging an intellectual and evanescent vacuum in popular culture, the whole concept of Air Instrumentation is no longer a risible phantasm but serves to underscore the fundamental politicization of an acrimonious dialectic in contemporary society."*

---

*We have no idea what this means. We even tried translating it into French or German. Still not a clue.

Luckily many traditional forms of Air Music live on. The Greek Army still includes the Ozone Air Band featuring the All-Air Bazouki Brigade. Touring troupes of Air Cossacks gallop across the frozen Steppes to this day waving their Air Balalaikas. In the British Isles traditional Air Music has survived in the bars of Western Ireland. Brendon O'Loon, the great Air Accordion player, has just recorded an acoustic album with Miles O'Toole, the popular young Air Fiddler. While in Edinburgh the All-Air Ceilidh Band (pronounced awll airr kalee banned) are artists in residence at the Royal Academie Ecosse in Morningside.

But perhaps most exciting of all is that with the rise in affordable, digital technology, more and more Air Musicians are exploring traditional forms in the comfort of their own homes.

THE HEALTH BENEFITS

*T*his book is all about better living. No matter what style you choose your mental and physical health will benefit in ways you never thought possible. Many Air Guitarists shed unwanted pounds and increase their cardio-vascularity within days of starting their exciting new hobby. They notice that their self-esteem and self-confidence doubles or triples within a few months of beginning to play. Moreover a recent Dutch study shows that significant enlargement of the male genitalia* is unavoidable. Dr Willi Dikisgroen measured astonishing growth in subjects playing Air Guitar in contrast to a control group who read handicraft magazines and experienced minor shrinkage. Although female Air Guitarists have shown huge growth in libido and reduction in hip measurement, enlargement in breast size proved negligible. A Swedish study proved inconclusive but really fun to do. Subjects found that breast enlargement did take place using a special soap while singing in the shower.

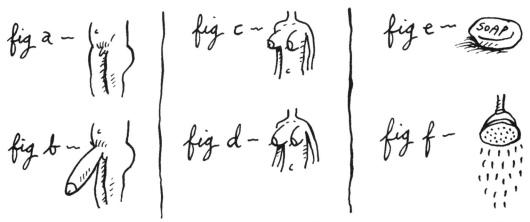

Perhaps the most significant health benefit is in the area of mental wellness. Playing Air Guitar has a profound effect on the mental state of everyone who tries it. Doctors are beginning to prescribe Air

---

*Mr Mole and Mr Appleby have no wish to offend, therefore the more modest reader should, if necessary, cut out an appropriately sized fig leaf and place it over any part of the drawing, above, which they find distasteful.

Guitar as a treatment for depression. International pharmaceutical companies are concerned that Air Guitar will replace many of their drugs. Soon Air Guitar will be available on the National Health. In Denmark and Holland doctors already use Air Guitar to help patients recover from back surgery and heart attacks. In Australia flying doctors bring Air Guitar deep into the Bush. Witch doctors in Nigeria use Air Guitar in many folk cures. Air Guitar is the key to unlocking the power of the imagination. Air Guitar has helped this man re-imagine his amputated arm.

It's a miracle! Now I can play Stairway To Heaven!

Still doubtful? Try this simple experiment:

1 - Close your eyes.

2 - VISUALIZE yourself stepping onto the stage of a giant stadium.

3 - FEEL the love of the crowd.

4 - HEAR the roar of their adulation.

5 - SMELL the cheap perfume, hormonal secretions and illegal drugs.

6 - SENSE the roadie handing you your favourite instrument.

7 - STRIKE that first power chord ...

Now open your eyes. Feel better? Of course you do. It's only natural. You just sent endorphins racing through you body, lowered your blood pressure and increased your life expectancy by ten minutes.

DIAGRAM SHOWING THE EFFECT OF IMAGINARY ADULATION ON HEAD SIZE:

BEFORE –

AFTER –

Thank you, thank you, thank you! You've been great...

NOTE HEAD TURNING PURPLE & ENGORGED WITH SELF-IMPORTANCE.

AIR ADDICTS

*B*ut it's not all positive. Sometimes even an innocent hobby can get out of control. In his book *12 String to 12 Step*, Dieter Mutter tells the harrowing story of his descent into Air Addiction:

"First I was playing the Air Guitar then the Air Drums, then any instrument of the orchestra was fair game for my obsession. I lost my dog, my girlfriend, even my partner in a lucrative business enterprise. I tried to cut it out but I enjoyed it too much."

Dieter was forced to try a version therapy.

"I could not afford real therapy, just a version of it. I stopped my ears. I tied my hands to the bed with copper wire. I wore lead shoes to stop the rhythm from invading my toes. Nothing was working. Nothing."

So how did Dieter escape his fate?

"I admit that I am powerless! So I change girlfriend, get new dog, find another business companion and start playing Air Football! Now I am fit, I am happy and I am not playing with myself. My team is in the Air Soccer Finals! We are winning and we have no balls. Life is Good!"

ALTERNATIVE INSTRUMENTAL REALITY

*T*o many devotees of the art, Air Guitar requires a substitute. This is known as:

Alternative

Instrumental

Reality

For these Air Musicians the urge to indulge in Air Play strikes around specific inanimate objects. Who among us has not been gripped by the need to play *Stairway To Heaven* on a common household broom? A cardboard tube of architectural blueprints is often all the temptation we need: a quick duckwalk around the office can easily lead to *Too Much Monkey Business*.

"Transformational iconography, deputational expression and alternative objectification, are all important subsets of the main group of imaginative, but non-originating, melodio-percussive role play."

(Dr Julian Fantone, Phd, again)

In other words, using something instead of a guitar.

SOME PROPS:

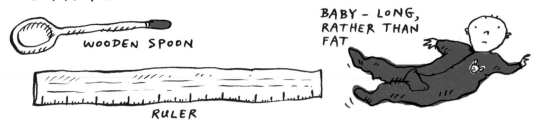

WOODEN SPOON

RULER

BABY - LONG, RATHER THAN FAT

Other objects suitable for transformation include: vacuum cleaners; squeezee mops (the traditional mop works far better as a bass); medium-sized dogs; cats; toddlers (up to age 28 months); chainsaws; ficus, aspidistras or other indoor foliage (avoid succulents or cacti); yardsticks; rulers; even firearms (though NEVER play rhythm guitar with a fully automatic weapon. Lance corporal Biggs claimed he was only playing *Brown Sugar* but the court martial ruled otherwise).

"That ain' righ'! Air Guitar means you got nuthin', not no broom handle, no mule stick, no fence picket. You ain' s'pose to have nuthin'. That's how come they calls it Air. Playing real Air Guitar takes skill and 'magination. Anybody can play a broom. Damn, you might as well play a real instrument an' all that takes is practice."

(Blind Lemon Pledge)

We respectfully disagree. Whatever inspires you is all right. You could even use a real guitar, although that defeats the purpose. Air Guitar is about Freedom. If you can get by with just your imagination, that's fine. But if you need a prop, that's fine too. We must rise above these barriers. This prejudice has split our community for too long.

THE BROOMSTICK CONTROVERSY

*L*ast year's vicious conflict in Finland between the Boothroyds and Skank re-ignited the controversy. Skank, New Jersey Air Punks, were in their first competition. As we all know, the Garden State breeds rock 'n' roll purists, willing to fight for their music. When the Boothroyds, a venerable Air Tribute Band from Eastern Ohio, took the stage with their trademark broomsticks, Skank assaulted them. Although the surprised buckeyes were driven into the wings, they were soon vigorously defending their honour. The East Coast Punks, wielding Air Chains and Sticks, were badly beaten by the Boothroyds' custom-made broomsticks. By the time Finnish riot police had broken up the brawl the Boothroyds had broken their precious instruments. Skank's drummer, Vic Spackle, had the last intact stick surgically removed two days later and has been forced to play standing up ever since.

SKANK POSING SHORTLY BEFORE ALL HELL BROKE OUT.

In the finals, b'reft of their b'sticks, the B'royds had to use locally manufactured substitutes. Their performance was a cruel joke, a pale shadow of their former glory. The members of Skank chose to perform a mocking copy of the Boothroyds' set using toilet brushes – a needless provocation, for which they won third place, behind Blood Fungus and The Menstruals.*

The other controversy at the Käymijärvi Stadium was the disqualification of the fourth-place winners in the lip-synching competition. The Boiler Sisters were discovered to be actually singing, while using the sound system to drown out their own voices. Even though they did not place in the medals their flaunting of the rules has removed them from international competition for two years. This kind of thing just spoils it for everybody.

---

*Blood Fungus and The Menstruals are in fact two separate groups. Blood Fungus is a hard-driving, "First Nations", band of speed metal freaks from Brantford, Ontario. The Menstruals is an all-female band hailing from Redondo Beach in Southern California.

CHORD CHARTS

*T*ake a look at these! Pretty impressive, right? Look at each chord for just five seconds and the special inks used to print this page will brand the chord pattern into your brain cortex. Too good to be true? Next time you reach for your Air Guitar you'll be twice as ready.

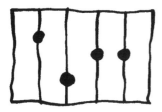

A major chord

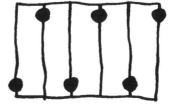

A blunt chord

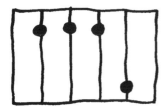

Not such A major chord

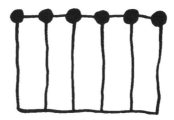

A really sharp chord

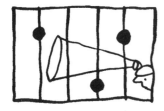

A miner

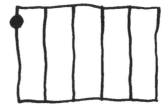

Another minor chord but less sharp

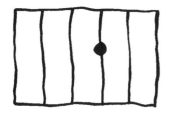

A quite dull chord

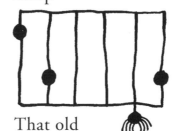

That old fuddy duddy E major

51

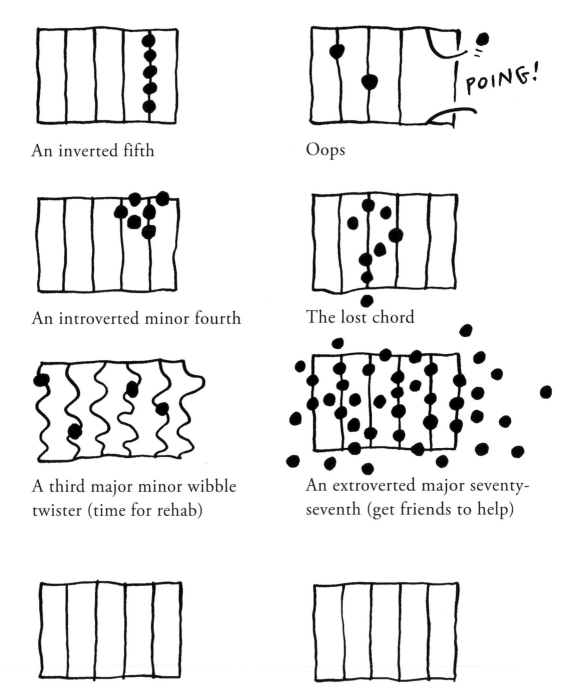

An inverted fifth

Oops

POING!

An introverted minor fourth

The lost chord

A third major minor wibble twister (time for rehab)

An extroverted major seventy-seventh (get friends to help)

Finally, how about making up a few chords of your very own? It's easy! Simply draw some round spots on the blank chord charts above. Now, place your fingers on the right strings and strum. Mmm ... Interesting.

AIR SHEET MUSIC

Study the sheet music overleaf for a moment. Looks complicated, doesn't it? Utterly incomprehensible? Yup. Well, relax. It's unintelligible to us, too. And that's intentional! It's meant to look impressive because the great thing about Air Sheet Music is you don't have to know how to read music. YOU JUST PRETEND TO READ IT! And notice there's no title? That's because this one pages fits all, from Beatles to Beethoven. Go on, wow your friends. Pop it onto your music stand and start playing note perfect instantly!

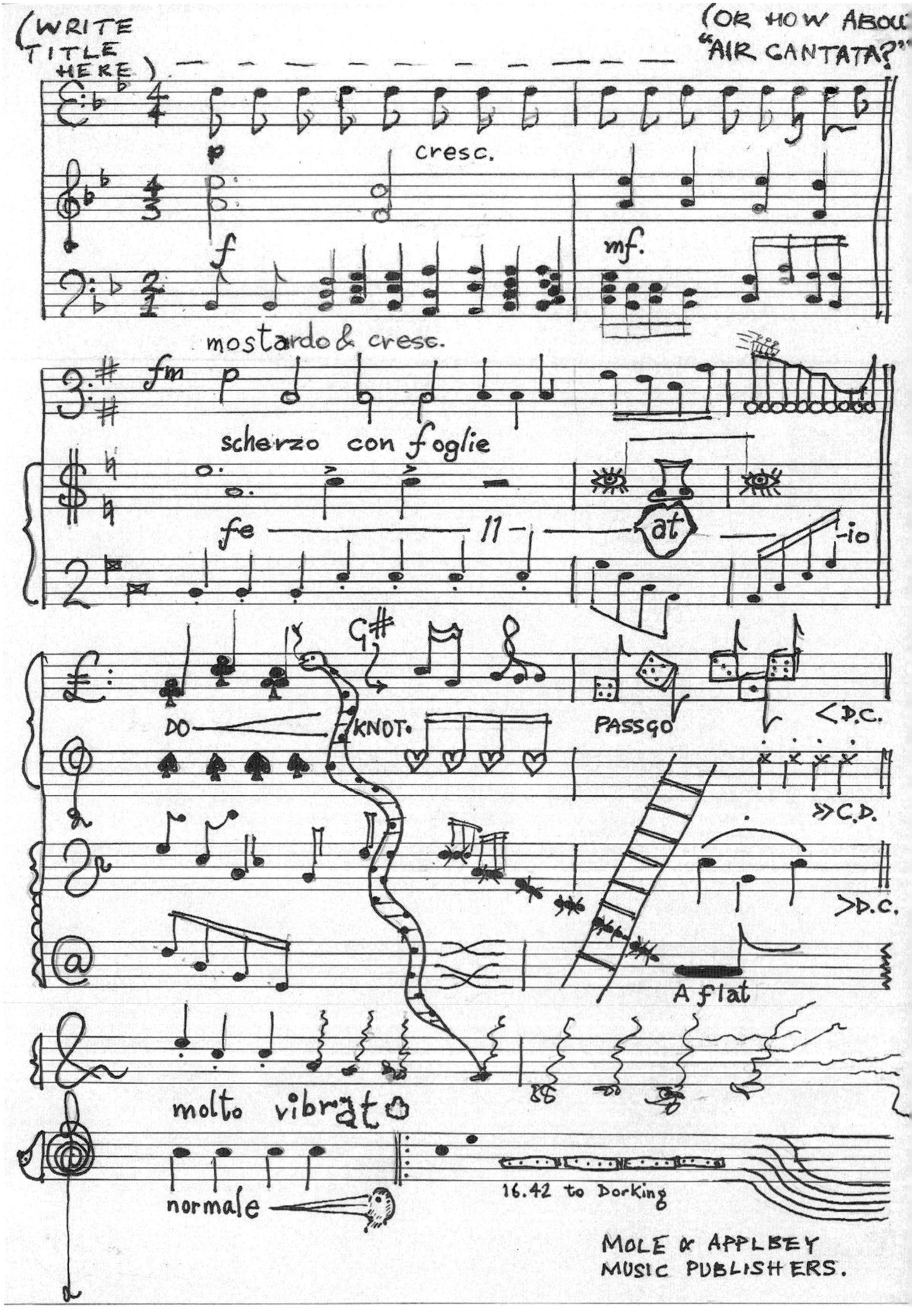
(WRITE TITLE HERE)
(OR HOW ABOU
"AIR CANTATA?"
cresc.
p
f
mf.
mostardo & cresc.
fm
scherzo con foglie
fe — ll — at — io
G#
DO
KNOT.
PASSGO
<D.C.
>>C.D.
>D.C.
A flat
molto vibrato
normale
16.42 to Dorking
MOLE & APPLBEY
MUSIC PUBLISHERS.

NEW HORIZONS

So you've done rock 'n' roll and are ready for a change. Why not try classical music?

First, a few things you MUST know:

1 - It's called an ORCHESTRA not a band.
2 - DO NOT applaud and shout "yeah" after the oboe solo.
3 - DO NOT shout "BEETHOVEN ROCKS!" randomly during a concert.
4 - DO NOT wave your lighter in the air during the last movement.
5 - NO head-banging, even during Wagner.
6 - And NEVER, however large the temptation, play Air Violin during the concert. Really, this is not okay.

The greatest thing about classical music is the number of instruments. Air Violin is really cool. You can go Gypsy, you can go Serious, Baroque, Romantic, even Light Classical/Easy Listening which is pretty uncool but it's your life, so go for it if that's your thing, we're not here to judge. Then there's oboe, clarinet, cor anglais – all pretty much the same. Turn sideways and purse your lips and you've got a flute or, if you're on air economy, a piccolo.

AIR FLUTE

NOTE THE SMART CLOTHES. NO JEANS AND T-SHIRT HERE.

Then press your lips together as if you were going to make some weird kind of farting noise and you've got the brass section: trumpets (cool!); French horn (note the strange hand position, right up the bell, kind of sexy); tuba (big!) and trombone (the Cadillac of Air Brass!). You've got everything you could want in a trombone: tooting/parping/sliding noises, pursed lips and major arm action.

SOME USEFUL LIP TIPS:

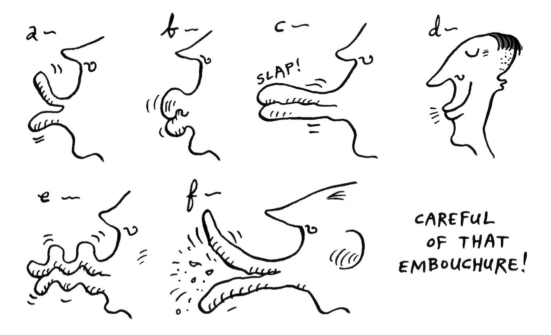

CAREFUL OF THAT EMBOUCHURE!

A BIG BAND AIR TROMBONE PLAYER (A LONG RIGHT ARM HELPS).

MAKE THIS THING, WHATEVER IT'S CALLED, FROM A BIG CARDBOARD BOX AND LOTS OF GLITTER.

But don't forget the strings: violin (nuff said); try viola for a change; double bass (slips between classical and jazz very smoothly! Nice); cello (is that a fantasy instrument, or what?!).

Here's Signor Coglioni, founding member of Il Conservatorio Della Aria and leading gastronomist, on playing the Air Cello:

"Seize your imagin-ed instrumental as you would the nak-ed womans. Grasp her neck, then stroke your tumescent bow firmly across her voluptuous mid-sectional. Make her melt in the hands like butter on the thighs of a goddess. Listen most carefully to her sounds, waiting for her crescendo, then carry her to the climax. At last put her gently to bed in the leather case, ready for the next time, when desire strikes."

Then there's all the percussion instruments: timpani (Italian for kettle drums) which make a great "BAU-OM" sound; snare drums ("rumtittumtum"); cymbals ("PSSHH"); triangle (the perfect "ting" of irony. A simple punctuation in the maelstrom of the symphony that is life.)

INSPIRATIONAL INTERLUDE

*T*hese rather bad photographs show Mr Appleby playing just a few of the many Air Instruments in his vast collection. Note the Air Oud hanging on the wall behind Mr A. I hope you can see clearly enough to make out his skillful fingering. In order to save the cost of a real photographer the pictures were taken by Mr Mole, which explains their poor quality. We're not made of money, you know. At least, not until this book sells more copies than the one you're holding right now.

Fig a: **Air Tuba** – Think: Oompah, oompah. There's not much more to it, really.

Fig b: **Air Piccolo** – Think: Tweed-lee-dee, but in a very high voice.

Fig c: **Air Trombone** – Think: In and out, in and out. Please use a lubricant and remember to clean your instrument.

Fig d: **Air ... er ...** – Mr Appleby has forgotten what he is playing in this picture. Air Notebook, perhaps?

And finally the ultimate Air Instrument of all time: the baton (which is French for *stick*). The conductor is an Air Musician on the very highest level. You get to stand up in front of a hundred people in dinner jackets and tell them what to do using just a stick! And some conductors don't even use a stick! Guess what? They just use their hands! Oh yes, my friend, the conductor whips them along like a herd of cattle! This is a whole real-life career in Air Music! And how hard can it be?

A TRADITIONAL
AIR BATON:

OR HOW ABOUT IMAGINING SOMETHING
A BIT MORE EXTRAVAGANT, SUCH AS
THIS SWISHY LITTLE NUMBER:

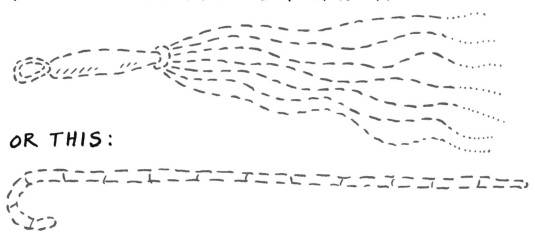

OR THIS:

THINGS TO KNOW:

1 - Tempi is Italian for faster or slower. Speeding up and slowing down is a major conductor thing. He is like the accelerator.

2 - It doesn't count if you don't sweat. These guys really work out. A symphony can last for a really long time. This is the real thing. Nothing phoney there!

3 - Wear cool clothes. Preferably tails.

4 - Treat your fellow musicians with contempt or at least patronizing condescension. They love it! Don't forget, you're the MAN.

5 - Conductors live for a really, really long time so get ready to enjoy life and travel all over the world.

Don't worry, you can still use all the facial gestures you learned earlier – THE SMUG, THE VOMIT, THE ORGASM – they work just as well for Mozart as they do for the Stones. You can't move around so much but that's okay because you can really concentrate on standing in front of the mirror working on your arm gestures. Try it out and pretty soon you'll be saying, "Classical music rocks!" (Just don't shout it out during the concert, this is definitely NOT O.K., O.K?)

CLASSICAL AIR GUITAR
You'll need a stool, and a very little stool – see picture opposite – or an office chair and two dictionaries will do. Bend over your instrument using the BREAM pose, so that you can see the fret board (the chord bit) and the sound hole (the hole where sound comes out). The audience should be able to see the bald spot on the top of your head.

BALD SPOT.

AN UNUSUAL PICTURE OF A REAL GUITAR BEING PLAYED BY AN AIR MUSICIAN.

1 - Start slowly using the very low notes.
2 - Use all fingers in a spider-like motion, as if tickling a favourite
     pussy under the neck.
3 - Quickly move to higher notes.
4 - When finished the first bit, smile benevolently, look myopically
     at the audience and start the next movement (sort of like the
     next track).

You can end the whole concert by standing slowly and bowing
slightly from the waist. Be cool.

Classical guitar is used a lot in TV advertisements and films shot in
exotic locations. Classical guitar music is often written by
composers no one has ever heard of so you're pretty safe if you
want to talk about them.

AIR FLAMENCO

Using this same set up you can enter the exciting and erotic world of flamenco. You get to play for angry gypsies who stamp their feet faster than a hummingbird beats its wings. They also sing very strange mournful songs about love, revenge and death in Spanish. It's powerful stuff. You get to eat tiny little pieces of food and drink sherry – a bit like going to your Gran's but with angry gypsies.

AIR FADO

The Portuguese version of the blues. It looks a bit like flamenco but don't say that or the Portuguese will kill you. The main instrument is the guitarra which isn't a guitar. Singers sing beautiful, sad songs about wanting to be somewhere else or wishing you were in love with someone else or sorry that it isn't still yesterday. You're doomed to wallow in nostalgia. It makes for great music.

IS G.A.G. GONE? IS GLAM AIR GUITAR DEAD OR JUST RESTING?

*T*ime was when Glam Air Guitar was the cutting edge, so sharp it sliced on contact. Way back in the 70's Glam Air Guitar burst out of the closet, then into the bedsit, where it preened in front of the mirror, put on eye make-up, platform shoes and strutted out into a crazy world of uppers and mirror balls. Then suddenly everyone wanted tight jeans, a great haircut and a good lick. Boys and girls of every color and creed, in every combination of genders and persuasions, were on the floor bumpin' and jivin', rockin' and boppin'. Disco and Glam brought us all out. We had no shame. We let it all hang out. Yes, there we were, under the multi-colored lights, all prancing about, showing off, getting down, picking it, strumming it, playing along. Yes, out into the seething swirl of sweating souls sashayed Glam Air Guitar in all its glory. We were all playing. We were all guilty. Was there no greater expression of freedom than a Public Display of Air Guitar? (P.D.A.G.)

LIONEL CHECKS HIS HAIR & MAKE-UP IN THE MIRROR BALL.

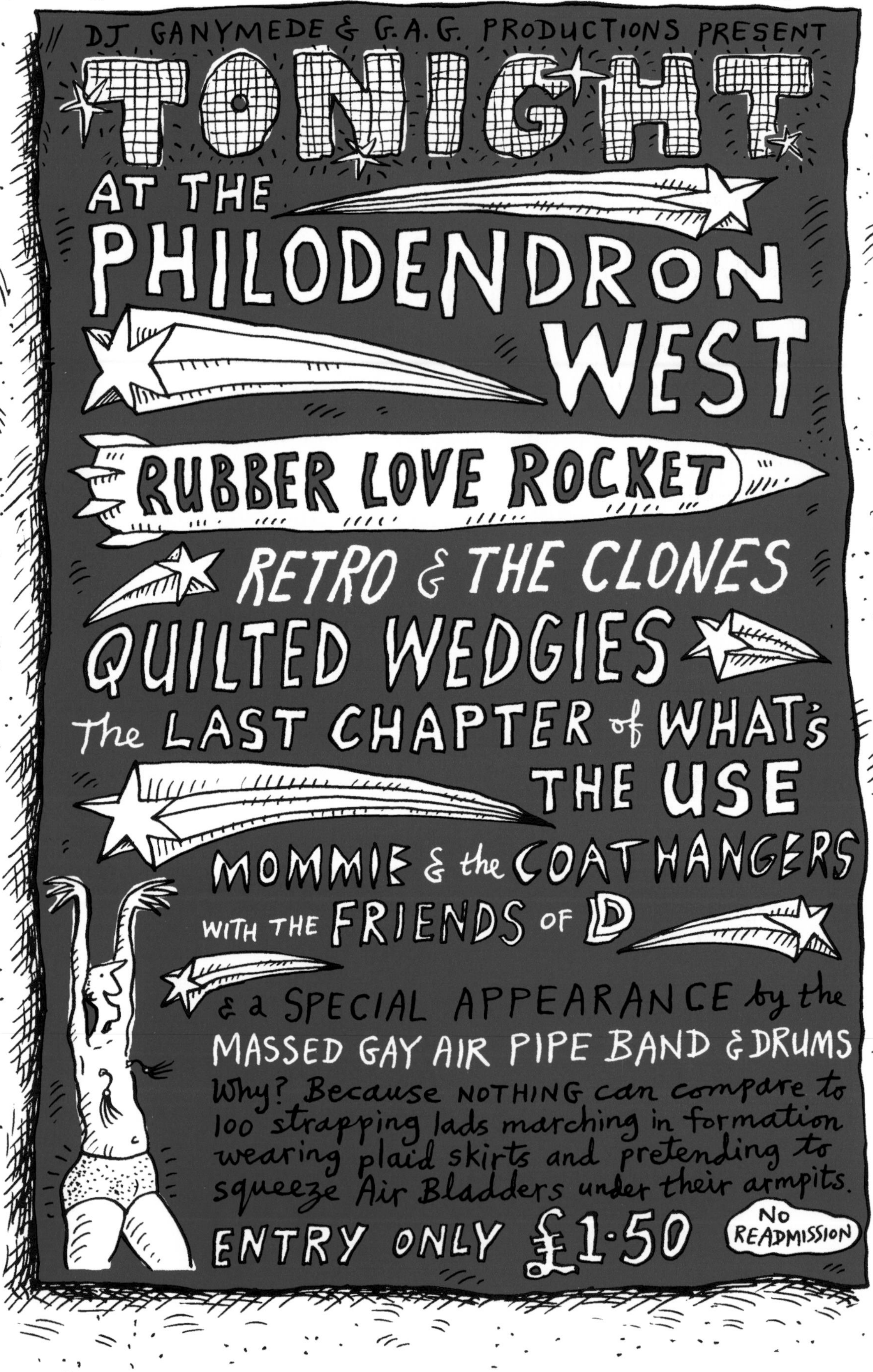
DJ GANYMEDE & G.A.G. PRODUCTIONS PRESENT
TONIGHT
AT THE
PHILODENDRON WEST
RUBBER LOVE ROCKET
RETRO & THE CLONES
QUILTED WEDGIES
The LAST CHAPTER of WHAT's THE USE
MOMMIE & the COAT HANGERS
WITH THE FRIENDS OF D
& a SPECIAL APPEARANCE by the
MASSED GAY AIR PIPE BAND & DRUMS
Why? Because NOTHING can compare to 100 strapping lads marching in formation wearing plaid skirts and pretending to squeeze Air Bladders under their armpits.
ENTRY ONLY £1·50
NO READMISSION

And the bands! Remember the great Glam Air Guitar bands? Take a look at this poster (left) from the height of the craze ...

Those were the nights! Doesn't it all make your mascara run with tears of nostalgia? What happened? Where did it all go? Are those days of flamboyance and fun gone forever?

Certainly not! You can have a Glam Theme Air Guitar Party in your very own home! But you will need authentic gay people to help you with the ambience. Even if you're as straight as a slidehammer and you live in Boresville, you can still invite that nice same-sex couple from down the street. And who knows? They might even redecorate the living room, do your taxes and replace your air filter. Gay people are multi-talented, productive members of society, as well as full of fun and artistic expression. So go on, push aside the loveseat, put the coffee table in the loft and send the kids to Auntie Pam. They don't need to see this kind of thing yet. (Alternatively, DON'T send the kids to Auntie Pam. This is EXACTLY the kind of thing they need to see.*)

Party on! Who says Glam is dead?

RECREATE THE GLITTERY DAYS OF GLAM WITH THESE DRESSING-UP TIPS!

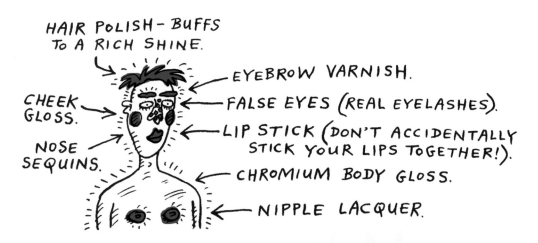

HAIR POLISH - BUFFS TO A RICH SHINE.

EYEBROW VARNISH.

FALSE EYES (REAL EYELASHES).

CHEEK GLOSS.

LIP STICK (DON'T ACCIDENTALLY STICK YOUR LIPS TOGETHER!).

NOSE SEQUINS.

CHROMIUM BODY GLOSS.

NIPPLE LACQUER.

*Delete according to how liberal you think you are.

AIR GODDESS

"If the devil has all the best tunes, why should men be the ones to play them?"

Sammi O'Rourke
(Rock Goddess and
part-time sales assistant)

*M*ost men reading this imagine women in rock as sex puppets, arm candy or stress relief. Come on, men, it's the 21st Century! LET THE OBJECTIFICATION CEASE! Enough! It is time! Women of Rock, unite! Stoke the flames of rebellion! Breathe the breath of fire! Let your volcano erupt! Release your inner Air Goddess!

In ancient times, Woman ruled the world. The High Priestess dominated the puny male sex, picking and choosing Her mates like cocktail nuts. And it was She who decided what music should be played. Look to your ancient past for inspiration! This pottery shard depicting the Minoan Goddess of Fertility plucking her Air Lyre and trampling on the discarded bodies of her lovers shows you what to do.

Men have usurped your power for too long. Take back the music! You don't need to go out to have a good time! You don't need a man to rock your world. So stay at home tonight and rock your own planet using the **GUITAR-GIRL GUIDE**, below:

BEGIN BY SHUTTING THE CURTAINS AND BOLTING THE DOOR ...

MAKE-UP:

None

Too much

CLOTHING:

vinyl, spandex, leather, anything too tight (Remember to use baby powder when wearing man-made textiles)

AMBIENCE

FOOD: a big box of choccies. Be your own Black Magic woman!

DRINK: Something life quenching. Howzabout a *Waterloo Sunset* (voddy and orangeade) or a *Smoke On The Water* (Baileys and Coke)

LIGHTING: low with a cheap Ikea spotlight, or use the emergency torch from under the stairs

PREPARATION

KIDS:

MAN:

Yes? Get rid of him. Send him out into the power of the totally stupid – his mates – to watch *Match of the Day* or grainy she-male porn

No? Don't start now!

Yes? Get rid of the little buggers. Send them on a bus to Grannie's house and if they don't have a Grannie, tell them to find one. If all else fails, dose them with cough syrup and sit them in front of a violent video game*

No? You don't need one, girl! Oh, all right. Use your imagination if you must

NOW TAKE SOME TIME FOR YOURSELF!

TURN IT ON!

CRANK IT UP!

LET IT ALL HANG OUT!

*NOTE: The above suggestions relating to children are made in the spirit of fun and hyperbole: they are in no way intended as real solutions to the problem of childcare. You might try calling a local teenager, needy relative or licensed professional. We are in no way condoning the mistreatment or abandoning of your offspring. But you have to admit it's a tempting thought.

(And when you've finished,
turn it off, shut it down and
cram it all back in before
you frighten someone)

Certificate of
AIR-WORTHINESS

KRANG... Am...

Congratulations...

YOU _____
(YOUR NAME HERE)
HAVE SUCESSFULLY COMPLETED AND
PASSED THE **APPLEBY** & **MOLE**
PRACTICAL COURSE IN **AIR GUITAR**
(ADVANCED LEVEL).

AWARD YOURSELF GRADE
1☐ 2☐ 3☐ 4☐ 5☐ 6☐ 7☐ 8☐ OTHER☐*

*Oh, go on! Why stop at
grade 8? Award your-
self grade 10. Or 12.
Or 88!

YOU ARE WORTHY!

George Mole
G. MOLE

Steven Appleby.
S. APPLEBY

FORMING YOUR OWN AIR BAND

*N*ow you've graduated with honours it's time to put your new-found skill to use. An Air Band is a big responsibility, like a goldfish, but you can't ask your Mum to flush a band down the toilet when it dies, so think carefully ... And then leap feet first into the Great Unknown that is Life!

Begin by putting up a notice at a local educational establishment or newsagent:

```
AIR BAND AUDITIONS!
DO YOU LIKE _____?(1)
SO DO WE.
LOOKING FOR LEAD GUITARISTS,(2) BASS,
DRUMS and KEYBOARDS.
CALL _____(3) OR BE AT _____ AT 4.30(4)
```

1 - Insert the band or style of your choice, e.g. Stones, Jamiroquai, Heavy Metal, Glam, Techno or Big Hair and Spandex. However perverse your musical tastes might be, you'll find kindred spirits out there.

2 - Don't bother to ask for rhythm guitarists. Try having two guitarists taking turns at lead. This will create much needed tension in the band and lead to the kind of fireworks, recriminations and tearful scenes of reconciliation that are so much a part of band life.

3 - Don't give your own number. You don't want a bunch of weirdos calling your house. Besides, leaving a strange number where it's difficult to leave a message adds an aura of mystery and authenticity to the whole enterprise.

4 - Hold auditions at a completely different time and place from the one given. Even on a different day. This will make a good story for the band biography and be COOL.

WHAT TO LOOK FOR

Lead guitarist: arrogance, flamboyant talent, and a polished exterior concealing a needy and frightened inner child.
Rhythm guitarist: look for another lead guitarist (see above – weren't you paying attention?).
Bass: look for anybody.
Drums: look for someone who can sit for hours without a chair. A sense of rhythm is preferred but not essential. Ask potential Air Drummers if they can say (a) Budda, budda, budda, budda, bang! (b) p-psh-tut, p-psh-tut, p-psh-tut ... This little test shows whether they can do loud or soft. If they can do both you've got "skins" (drums) and cymbals (round, metal things that go crash or psh).

NOTE: Beware. You may lose your Air Drummer to a rap group. Air Drummers are used to provide the rhythmic background to rappers' anger. If you want to pursue this career you need to get a microphone and concentrate on making explosive noises with pursed lips. Remember when you played Armies or War in the playground?

Keyboards: skill only limited by the number of imaginary synthesizers they can stack up. Your keyboard player should be able to play on any table, desk or horizontal surface.

Here we see Vladimir Pushpin playing on the back of a patient. He claims that Rach 3 point 1 (a cool way of saying the first movement of Rachmaninoff's Third Piano Concerto – it's a classical piece) can realign most spines. If deep tissue therapy is needed he goes on to the other movements. By the time he gets to the last movement the patient feels like jelly. You could try a little light techno or some country honky-tonk piano on your Dad and see if it helps his sciatica.

Singers: Do they look good? Do you fancy them? Do they fancy themselves? All these are important questions. Do not encourage them to actually sing. Most Air Singers are long on expression and short on pipes. Besides, if it turns out they really can sing they might get hijacked by a real band. It's bad enough you risk losing your drummer.

NAMING YOUR AIR BAND IS EASY WITH THE ROULETTE WHEEL OF NAME COMBINATIONS!

1. WRITE NOUNS IN THE OUTER CIRCLE (EG - FRUIT OR ANIMALS).
2. WRITE ADJECTIVES & VERBS IN THE MIDDLE CIRCLE (EG - FLYING OR DARK).

HERE'S ONE WE'VE DONE FOR YOU - OR MAKE YOUR OWN!

3. CLOSE YOUR EYES & RACE YOUR FINGERS AROUND THE PAGE UNTIL THEY STOP — JUST LIKE A ROULETTE BALL. OR CUT OUT THE HANDY SPINNER (BELOW) & PIN TO CENTRE OF PAGE.

GROUPIES AND ROADIES

*B*asically anyone who belongs to a group ending in *–ies* is your slave. Groupies and Roadies live to be slaves to the music and this makes you their god for a gig.*

They will do anything for you. And we mean anything. Whatever your demands Groupies and Roadies are an important part of your new life. Remember: where there are those bold enough to lead, there are those eager to follow. Take full advantage of those poor souls who crave a piece of your fame, real or imaginary, and put them to work.

A HUNCHED, HUNCHBACK AIR ROADIE TRIES TO SNEAK ACROSS THE STAGE WITHOUT BEING NOTICED TO UNTANGLE YOUR FOOT FROM MIKE'S LEAD AND ASSORTED GIRLS' PANTIES.

AIR ROADIES

*I*n the stadium of your imagination you are almighty. The roar of applause from your adoring disciples is deafening. Raise your hands to acknowledge their praise ... But wait!

- You want another guitar with two necks.
- The microphone is too low.
- You've decided to go acoustic.
- A crazed fan has grabbed your left ankle.

You need a roadie! The guardian angel of the rock god. Roadies are born, not made. Where, in the recesses of your imagination, can you find a roadie? Look into your past. How about your invisible childhood friend Bunty or a favourite superhero? Much-loved stuffed animals, such as your bear and rabbit, make great roadies. Also your best friend from when you were seven. Summon one of these characters from your past. They are used to your petty demands. They have already sworn allegiance to you. They are happy to be subservient. They long to do your bidding.

In this picture your stuffed rabbit, now grown up and high on drugs, changes a guitar string helped by your favourite superhero, CANKEROUSMAN, and a friend from childhood. A bear watches.

---

*Please note the use of the lower case "g." The authors of this work and their representatives do not wish to incur the wrath of the Deity or anyone claiming to speak for the Deity. Any fatwas or death threats by religious groups are hereby deemed unjustified. Rock god is only a figure of speech (see Irony).

AIR GROUPIES

*N*ow we stray into the minefield of intimate activity. Basically, after a hard driving concert you want someone who will cater to your every whim, however base or reprehensible.

AIR GROUPIE – NOTE NOZZLE FOR FILLING WITH AIR. ALSO AVAILABLE IN MALE VERSION WITH INFLATABLE PENIS.

CHARACTERISTICS:
Stretchy clothing, big hair, cheap perfume, mute, annoying laugh, pneumatic physique, boundless energy, morals so loose they blow away in a light breeze, free from disease, gender unimportant – this is an equal opportunity fantasy.

Classical groupies act like crazed bacchantes, tearing their quarry apart. Hordes of classical groupies can rip an entire orchestra to shreds like a shoal of piranha.

The derivation of the word groupie is obscure. Is it someone who follows a group, or someone who likes group sex? Or both? And why not a bandie or a rockie? Probably the most important attribute of a groupie is that they need to be unconcerned with your physical shortcomings.

AIROTIC SUBSTITUTION

*O*f course, if you and your life partner – or a consenting adult of like mind – wish to explore the amorous possibilities of Air Music, you can always play each other. Taking turns to be the instrument or the player can add new dimensions to a tired relationship. Before trying the suggested conjunctions on the following pages, please consult a physician or wear an Air Truss for greater comfort and safety. We hope you find these positions useful but not offensive.

Ooh! That
A sharp
diminished
fifth
really
tickles!

SUSAN PLAYS RALPH, WEARING THE DJANGO AIR TRUSS, WITH AN AIR WOBBLE-BOARD.

The Django Air Truss, pictured here in the deluxe sporting edition, allows you to pursue your hobby with confidence and ease. Your partner can be suspended from the aerial sling allowing you free use of both hands for maximum pleasure and playing potential.

THE GUITARMA SUTRA

Inverted Fish – laid back and easy for folk music.

Clasping Crab – disco inferno for your hunk a' burning love.

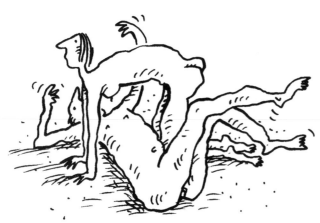

The Tiger's Bone Yard – a charming old standby. Try a sonata for lute or viola de gamba, or anything needing big hair and platform boots.

Electric Lotus – best
for the blues.

Yawning Frog – much needed
intimacy for speed metal freaks.

Reversed Candle –
a hard rock classic.

Wheelbarrow – an old
favourite for an evening
of rhythm 'n' blues.

CLASSICAL DEVIANCE

*T*he L.S.O. or London Substitution Orchestra has been combining classical music and sadomasochism for over forty years. The dominants play the submissives in long, gruelling symphonic concerts. Mr H. remained a double bass for three days. Before a concert the "instruments" are stripped naked and forced to lick the stage clean. Then the "musicians" play them for several hours. Afterwards the "instruments" are shut up in their cases while the "musicians" parade around the auditorium in opera capes drinking mulled schnapps.

The "conductor" is the ultimate dominant: he is expected to chastise the musicians and instruments in the orchestra verbally and physically, even during the concert. Not very different from life in most symphony orchestras really. Last year's concert, at the Stadt Theater Sadismuss in Dortmund, featured a rousing performance of Berlioz's Symphonie Fantastique – reviewed by the *Guardian* as "Berlioz, Berli-clothed" – and no less than three Mahler symphonies. It was a very long concert indeed. The first trombone suffered a groin pull, the entire wind section was hospitalized with tumescent embouchures and two cymbals were treated for percussion. The price of art is steep but when the other "instruments" were let out of their cases the next day, the expressions on their faces said it was all worth it.

THE ZEN OF AIR MUSIC

*I*n the time of the samurai, the power of Zen ruled. Japanese Zen masters could shoot arrows into the bull's eye blindfold. Blind swordsmen fought as many as fifty-seven opponents. Masters of the martial arts could throw their enemies without touching them. These same Zen masters could play instruments from across the room.

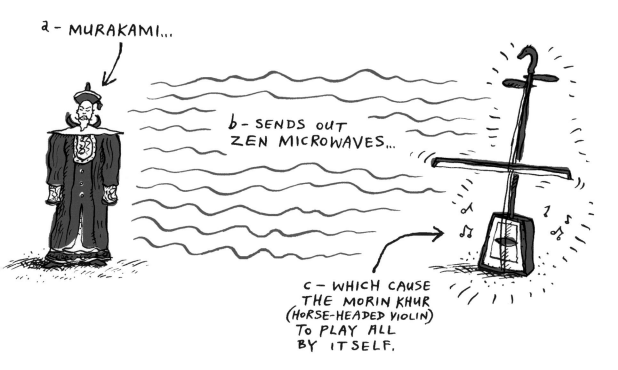

a – MURAKAMI...

b – SENDS OUT ZEN MICROWAVES...

c – WHICH CAUSE THE MORIN KHUR (HORSE-HEADED VIOLIN) TO PLAY ALL BY ITSELF.

In 1673, the great Murakami sat alone in his simple dwelling in the hills, while miles away the court listened to his samisen play an entire concert on its own. One day the Emperor decreed that Murakami should play for him and his mistress every day at noon. The Zen master would not leave his contemplation of a waterfall, yet every day at noon the Emperor and his mistress heard music. That music is now known as "Waterfall of the Mind Suite." After the Emperor died, five jealous court musicians banned Air Music and banished the great Zen master to the island of Rishiri-To. Despite this Murakami forced them to listen to the same song for 18 hours a day until they went mad.

By channeling the guitar greats you, too, can enter the world of Zen. You can "touch" the original guitar. You can be the conduit for the music. There is purity in Air Music that ordinary music can never achieve. The instrument and even the original player just get in the way. In fact, many professional musicians have switched to Air Music just to avoid all that unnecessary clutter. Just imagine the sense of freedom that Air Music can give someone who has been shackled to an instrument his whole life. Freedom from practicing, from rehearsals, from travel, from concerts, from the very Tyranny of Time!

Air Music can be enjoyed any time. You even don't need music to play Air Guitar. You can make your own music or just imagine. Think of the money you'll save on headphones. After all, music is more than just sound. It is first and foremost an experience of the mind, and don't we owe it to ourselves to listen to our own Symphonies of the Mind? Thanks to the power of Memory we can access our own music files whenever we want. You could be standing at a bus stop while you groove to some cool jazz. Waiting to check the overdraft while you listen to *Layla*. Sitting on the 5.47 while you're really on that *Midnight Special*. And when you get home – delays due to signal work – look up into the night sky and listen to the Music of the Spheres. Just stand back and watch the constellations rock out to the Air Music of the Universe!

APPENDIX

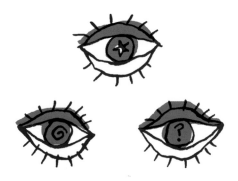

THE AIR CATALOGUE
Quality Air Items for fun, leisure and business use!

AIR BOOKS – Easy to carry. Many Great Classics available.
Suitable for nudists. To claim your FREE Air Edition of this book,
cut out the coupon below and hand in at your local bookshop where
you see the special display.

(Please note: your Air
Edition may not be
exchanged or bartered for this
paper edition due to
International Reuse and
Recycling Regulations.)

AIR-POD – Enjoy all your favourite sounds. Excellent accessory for
public transport – will not disturb other travellers. Never needs
recharging.

UNDERW-AIR – VPL is a thing of the past!
No visible seams or binding elastic. May be
worn under man-made vinyl accessories
without fear of combustion.

AIR
APPENDIX*

AIR MOBILE –
Talk to anyone,
anytime, anywhere.
No clumsy cords.
No annoying bills.
May be used safely
underwater.

*No need to worry
about Air Appendicitis.
Your Air Appendix
isn't there in the
first place.

AIR CAR – A full line of Air Vehicles (AV's) will soon be available. Enjoy full visibility. It's fun! It's comfortable! It's Free! *"It's like riding on Air!"* Because you are!

AIR BALLS – Amaze your friends with your juggling skills!

AIR UNICYCLE – Amaze your friends with your balancing skills! Why not combine these two products and enjoy a substantial discount? Tower above the traffic, entertain your fellow citizens, enjoy invigorating exercise on your commute.

AIR PETS – No mess, no fuss, just hours of devotion! (Please do not let your other pets mate with your Air Pet. Air Pet mixes can be unfulfilled and confused.)

THIS PAGE IS RESERVED FOR THE SOLE
USE OF MR MOLE & MR APPLEBY

In the event that you attend a book signing
it will be used by the authors to
personalise your volume.

If you are unable to attend a book signing, please
complete the two signatures, below, with a
quality writing implement of your choice.

Alternatively, you may use this page for writing
lists, comments, phone numbers, addresses and
other useful information.

Thank you.

George Mole

Steven Appleby

AIR QUIZ ANSWERS

1 - The one with his back to us. 2 - The drummer – as usual. He's only in the band because he owns a set of Air Drums.
3 - The bass player (back left). He can play fastest. 4 - Seven. Beware of air feedback. 5 - Synthesiser, obviously.
6 - Trick question. None of them are Bez. The lead singer is Bez's boyfriend.